In Search of Cryptids

In Search of Cryptids, Volume 1

Cassiel E. Nox

Published by Cassiel E. Nox, 2024.

IN SEARCH OF CRYPTIDS

First edition. November 15, 2024.

Copyright © 2024 Cassiel E. Nox.

ISBN: 979-8230763758

Written by Cassiel E. Nox.

Table of Contents

In Search of Cryptids VOLUME: I

Cassiel E. Nox

CASSIEL E. NOX
UNRAVELING SECRETS OF THE UNIVERSE

Welcome to "In Search of Cryptids: Vol I!"
Dear reader,

Thank you for choosing to embark on this journey with me. I am excited to share this story with you and hope it brings you as much joy and inspiration as it brought me while writing it. Whether you're a returning reader or visiting my work for the first time, I am truly grateful for your support.

If you enjoyed the book, please share your thoughts through a review or recommend it to your friends. Your feedback helps me improve and continue to bring stories to readers like you.

Happy reading!

With gratitude,

Cassiel E. Nox

Thank You

Unveiling the Enigma of Cryptids

Introduction

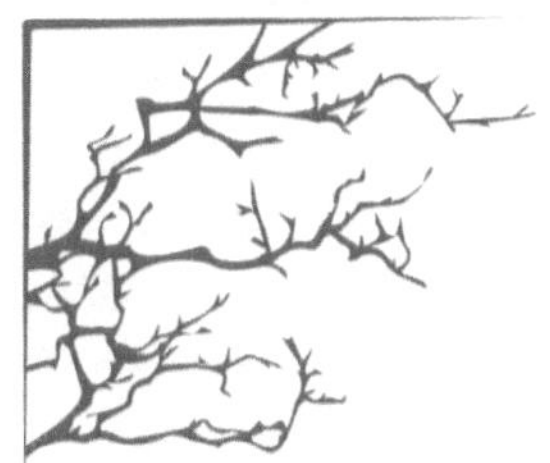

Throughout human history, tales of enigmatic creatures lurking just beyond the fringes of our understanding have captivated our imaginations. These elusive beings, known as cryptids, have left an enduring mark on folklore, literature, and popular culture. From the towering Bigfoot to the elusive Loch Ness Monster, cryptids have ignited our curiosity and fueled our speculations about the hidden wonders that may exist in the natural world.

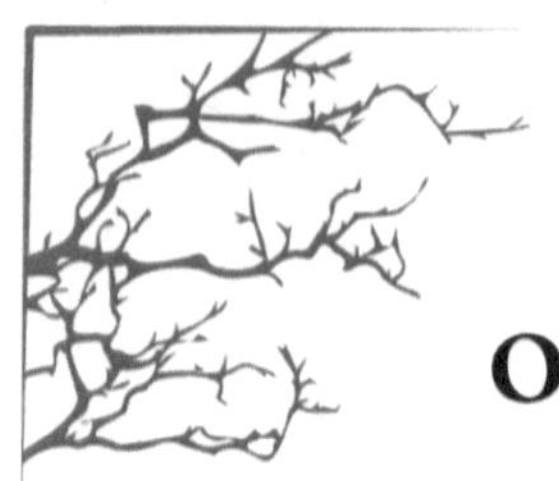

Origins and Definitions

The term "cryptid" was first coined by zoologist Bernard Heuvelmans in his 1955 book "On the Track of Unknown Animals." It refers to creatures that are claimed to exist but lack definitive scientific evidence to confirm their presence. Cryptids often inhabit the twilight zone between the known and the unknown, their existence supported by anecdotal evidence, eyewitness accounts, and intriguing physical traces.

Throughout human history, tales of enigmatic creatures lurking just beyond the fringes of our understanding have captivated our imaginations. These elusive beings, known as cryptids, have left an enduring mark on folklore, literature, and popular culture. From the towering Bigfoot to the elusive Loch Ness Monster, cryptids have ignited our curiosity and fueled our speculations about the hidden wonders that may exist in the natural world.

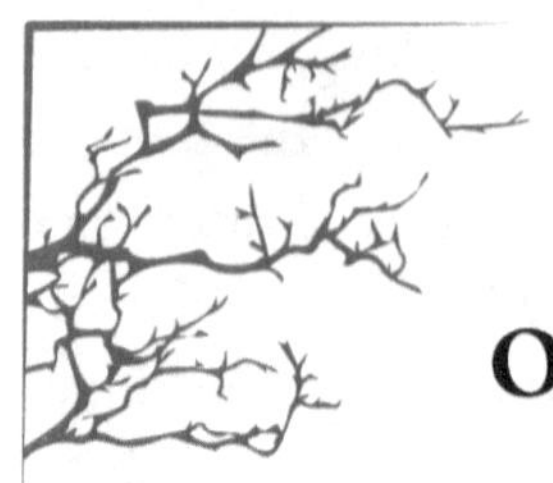

Origins and Definitions

The term "cryptid" was first coined by zoologist Bernard Heuvelmans in his 1955 book "On the Track of Unknown Animals." It refers to creatures that are claimed to exist but lack definitive scientific evidence to confirm their presence. Cryptids often inhabit the twilight zone between the known and the unknown, their existence supported by anecdotal evidence, eyewitness accounts, and intriguing physical traces.

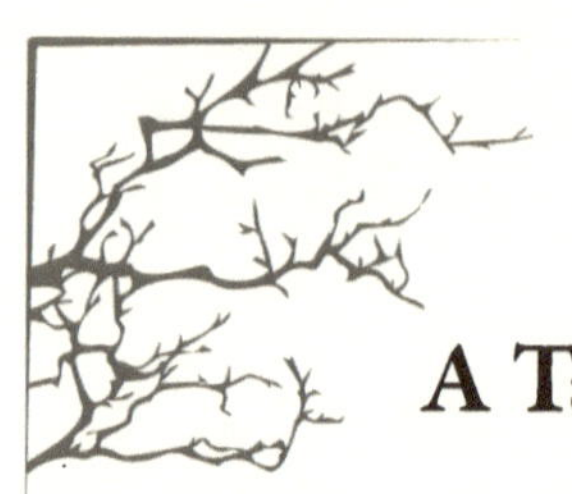

A Tapestry of Cryptid Lore

Cryptids are not confined to any particular region or era. They appear in the myths and legends of cultures worldwide, from the ancient tales of the Thunderbird among Native American tribes to the more recent sightings of the Chupacabra in the Americas. Each cryptid carries with it a unique set of characteristics, behaviors, and habitats, reflecting the diverse tapestry of human imagination and cultural beliefs.

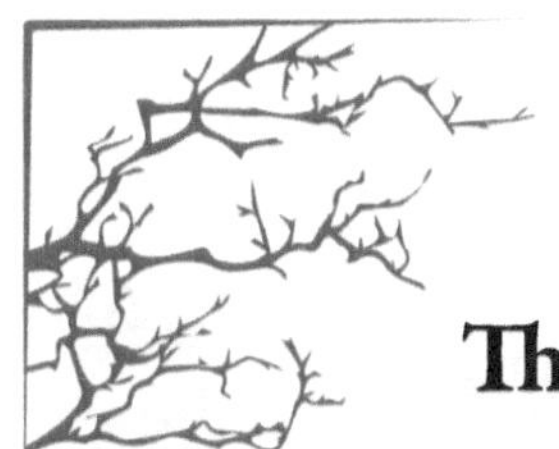

The Scientific Perspective

Despite the allure of cryptids, the scientific community generally maintains a cautious stance towards their existence. The lack of definitive evidence, such as clear photographs or physical specimens, makes it challenging to verify their presence. However, some scientists remain open to the possibility that cryptids could represent undiscovered species or phenomena that challenge our current understanding of the natural world.

The Enduring Fascination

Regardless of their scientific status, cryptids continue to capture the public's imagination. They embody our innate curiosity about the unknown and our desire to explore the boundaries of the possible. Cryptid enthusiasts form communities, organize expeditions, and share their experiences and theories in a vibrant subculture dedicated to unraveling the mysteries that surround these enigmatic creatures.

Exploring the Mysteries: Different Types of Cryptids

Cryptids, often sidelined to the realms of myth and legend, have fascinated humanity for centuries. These mysterious creatures, whose existence is suggested but not proven by scientific evidence, have been a part of cultural folklore worldwide. From the lush forests of North America to the icy heights of the Himalayas, tales of cryptids weave through the fabric of various cultures, adding an element of mystery and wonder to our understanding of the world.

The term 'cryptid' originates from the word 'cryptozoology,' a field that combines the Greek words 'Kryptos', meaning hidden, and 'zoology', the study of animals. This branch of study often operates on the fringes of mainstream science, focusing on animals that are rumored or believed to exist, yet lack concrete evidence. It encompasses well-known creatures like Bigfoot and the Loch Ness Monster and lesser-known entities such as the Bunyip or the Wendigo.

What drives our fascination with cryptids? Perhaps it is the allure of the unknown, the possibility that our world still holds secrets and undiscovered wonders. Cryptids also reflect our cultural beliefs and fears, embodying the mysteries of unexplored landscapes and the depths of human imagination. In folklore, these creatures often play roles that highlight moral lessons or explain natural phenomena, shaping societal norms and values. In modern times, cryptids have found a firm place in media and popular culture, from movies and books to video games and television series. These mysterious beings' stories and alleged sightings fuel our curiosity, often leading to detailed investigations and search expeditions. As we embark on this journey to explore different cryptids, we will dive into the origin stories, famous sightings, and the cultural impact of each creature; whether you are a skeptic or a believer, the intrigue and fascination these enigmatic beings evoke.

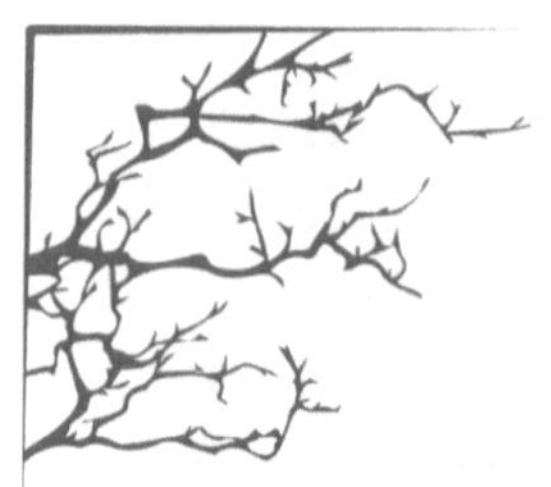

Bigfoot (Sasquatch)

Bigfoot, also known as Sasquatch, is one of North American folklore's most famous and enduring cryptids. Described typically as a large, hairy, bipedal humanoid, Bigfoot is said to inhabit forests, mainly in the Pacific Northwest region of the United States and Canada. Over the years, this creature has become a staple of popular culture, spawning countless books, films, and passionate debates among believers and skeptics alike. But what exactly is Bigfoot, and why has it captured the collective imagination for so long?

Bigfoot's descriptions vary, but most accounts depict a creature standing between 6 to 10 feet tall, covered in dark brown or reddish hair, with enormous feet, as its name suggests. The footprints attributed to Bigfoot range from 15 to 24 inches. Witnesses often report a strong, unpleasant odor accompanying sightings and describe the creature as having an ape-like face, deep-set eyes, and a prominent brow ridge.

The origins of Bigfoot stories can be traced back to Native American traditions, where several tribes have legends of giant, hairy creatures inhabiting the wilderness. The term 'Sasquatch' comes from the Halkomelem language of the Coast Salish people in British Columbia. These indigenous stories lend a cultural and historical depth to the Bigfoot legend, showing that the belief in such creatures predates modern accounts for centuries.

One of the most famous pieces of Bigfoot evidence is the Patterson-Gimlin film, shot in 1967 in Bluff Creek, California. The short clip shows a large, bipedal creature covered in hair walking along a creek bed. The film has been the subject of extensive analysis and debate, with some experts claiming it is a hoax, while others argue it provides compelling evidence of Bigfoot's existence. Despite the controversies, the Patterson-Gimlin film remains an iconic piece of cryptozoological history.

Over the decades, thousands of reported sightings and encounters with Bigfoot have occurred. These accounts often come from hikers, campers, and locals familiar with the areas where the creature has been spotted. Some of the more notable sightings include the 1924 'Ape Canyon' incident in Washington State, where a group of miners claimed several ape-like creatures attacked them, and the more recent sightings in the Appalachian Mountains and the forests of Oregon.

Scientists and researchers have conducted numerous investigations into the Bigfoot phenomenon. Physical evidence such as footprints, hair samples, and feces have been collected and analyzed. While some of these findings have been inconclusive or debunked as hoaxes, others remain unexplained. The field of cryptozoology, which studies hidden and unknown animals, continues to view Bigfoot as one of its most intriguing subjects.

B eyond the scientific community, Bigfoot has had a significant cultural impact. The creature has appeared in a wide variety of media, from the 1972 classic film The Legend of Boggy Creek to modern-day TV shows like Finding Bigfoot. This widespread presence in popular culture has helped keep the legend alive, inspiring new generations to explore and investigate the mystery.

Despite the lack of definitive proof, Bigfoot's allure endures. The possibility that such a creature could exist in the vast, uncharted wilderness captivates the human spirit of adventure and curiosity. Whether through serious scientific research or casual storytelling around a campfire, Bigfoot continues to be a fascinating and enigmatic figure in the world of cryptids.

In conclusion, Bigfoot is more than just a myth or a dubious legend; it represents a profound aspect of human culture and our relationship with the unknown. If there are dense forests and unexplored territories, the mystery of Bigfoot will continue to inspire, challenge, and intrigue us.

Loch Ness Monster

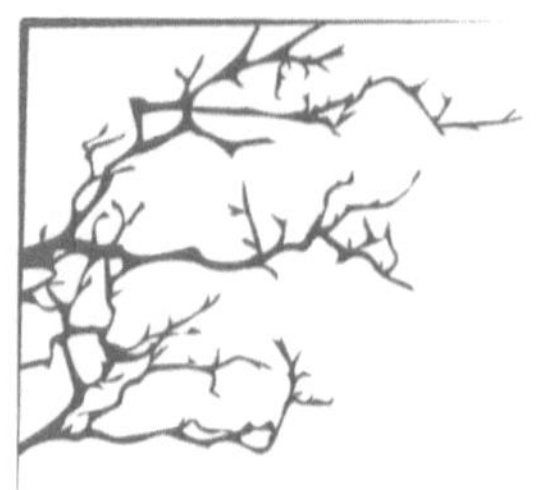

The Loch Ness Monster, affectionately known as Nessie, is one of the most famous cryptids in the world. Nestled deep within Scotland's Loch Ness, a large freshwater lake, Nessie has captured the imagination of locals and enthusiasts around the globe for centuries. Let's dive into this elusive creature's origins, famous sightings, scientific investigations, and cultural impact.

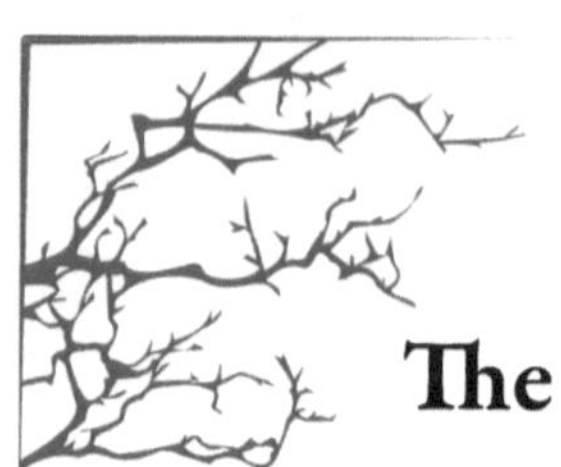

The Origin and Description

The tales of the Loch Ness Monster can be traced back to ancient times. The earliest written reference dates back to 565 AD, in the book 'Life of St. Columba', where it was described as a water beast attacking a man in the River Ness. Over time, the myth transformed, and Nessie became synonymous with the loch itself. Descriptions of the creature vary, but it is commonly depicted as a giant, long- necked sea serpent with one or more humps protruding from the water. Some describe it as resembling a Plesiosaur, a prehistoric marine reptile, which adds to its mystique.

Famous Sightings

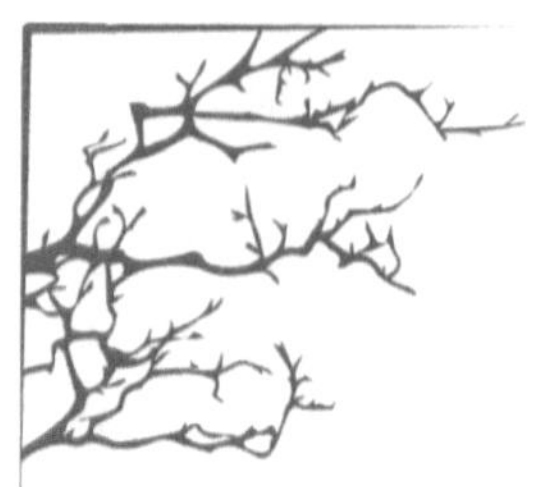

One of the most famous sightings occurred in 1933 when George Spicer and his wife claimed to have seen a gigantic creature cross the road before their car and disappear into the loch. They described it as having a large body and a long, wavy neck. This sighting ignited worldwide interest, and several more reports followed. In 1934, a London doctor, Robert Kenneth Wilson took what is known as the 'Surgeon's Photograph'. This blurry image, depicting a long neck and head rising out of the water, became iconic and is still one of the most recognized images associated with Nessie.

However, over the years, many have questioned the authenticity of these sightings and photographs. In 1994, it was revealed that the 'Surgeon's Photograph' was a hoax, involving a toy submarine with a sculpted head attached. Despite this, die-hard believers continue to search for concrete evidence of Nessie's existence.

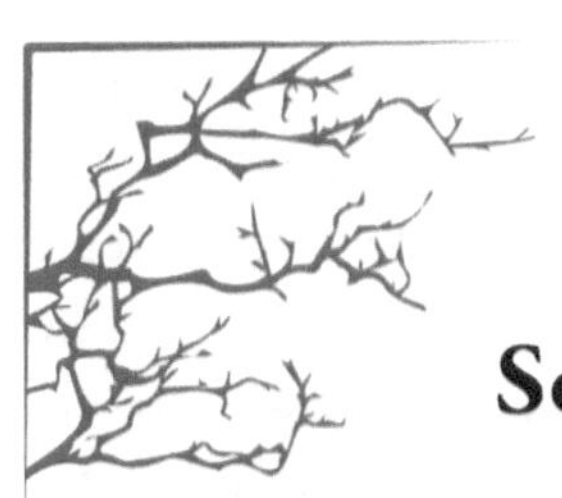

Scientific Investigations

Numerous scientific endeavors have been conducted to uncover the truth behind the Loch Ness Monster. One of the most notable investigations was Operation Deepscan in 1987. A fleet of boats equipped with echo-sounding equipment traveled across the loch, searching for any large, unusual objects underwater. The operation did pick up some unidentified sonar contacts, but nothing conclusive was found.

In recent years, geneticists have joined the hunt. In 2018, a team of scientists conducted a DNA survey of Loch Ness, extracting genetic material from water samples. They aimed to identify every living species in the loch to see if any unusual genetic markers could hint at the presence of an unknown creature. The results, published in 2019, debunked the Plesiosaur theory but did suggest that the sightings could be attributed to large eels populating the loch. Still, this has not stopped cryptid enthusiasts from believing Nessie might be out there.

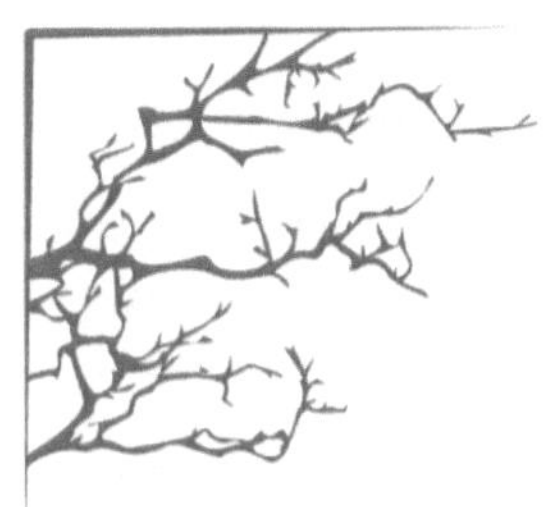

Cultural Impact

Nessie has left an indelible mark on popular culture. The Loch Ness Monster has inspired books, movies, television shows, and even music. From Sherlock Holmes's 'The Adventure of the Abbey Grange' to animated films like 'The Water Horse: Legend of the Deep', Nessie has found her way into various genres and storytelling traditions.

Moreover, the Loch Ness Monster has become a significant part of local tourism. Visitors flock to the Loch Ness area hoping to glimpse the mythical creature, boosting the local economy significantly. There are dedicated boat tours, visitor centers, and museums where enthusiasts can learn more about the creature and its rich history. This fascination with Nessie reflects the broader human penchant for mysteries and the unknown.

In conclusion, the legend of the Loch Ness Monster continues to thrive, fueled by a mix of historical accounts, tantalizing yet inconclusive evidence, and a deep-rooted desire to believe in something beyond the ordinary. While science may not have confirmed Nessie's existence, the cultural impact and the sense of wonder she inspires are undeniable.

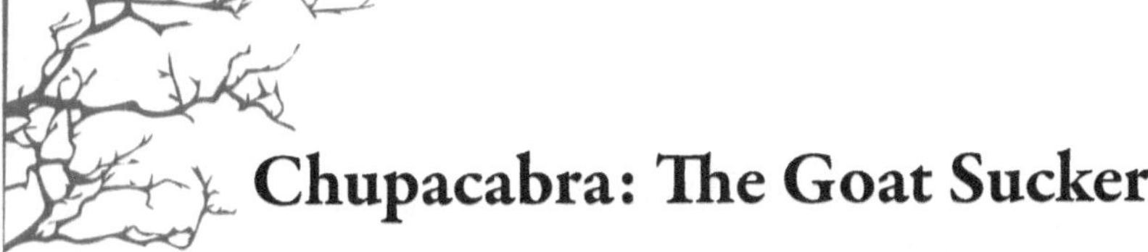

Chupacabra: The Goat Sucker

The legend of the Chupacabra, which translates to 'goat sucker,' is one of the most modern and enigmatic cryptid stories around. Born from the heartland of Latin America, particularly Puerto Rico, the Chupacabra has made its way into the annals of cryptid legends much faster than many of its older and more storied counterparts. Unlike Bigfoot or the Loch Ness Monster, the Chupacabra's tale began in the 1990s, making it a relatively recent addition to the cryptozoology Hall of Fame.

According to descriptions, the Chupacabra is a small, bear-like creature with a row of spines reaching from its neck to the base of its tail. Its skin is often described as leathery or scaly, with a distinct reptilian quality. The eyes of the Chupacabra are usually glowing red, which some believe adds to its terrifying visage. Witness reports have varied over the years, some describing it as a hopping creature like a kangaroo.

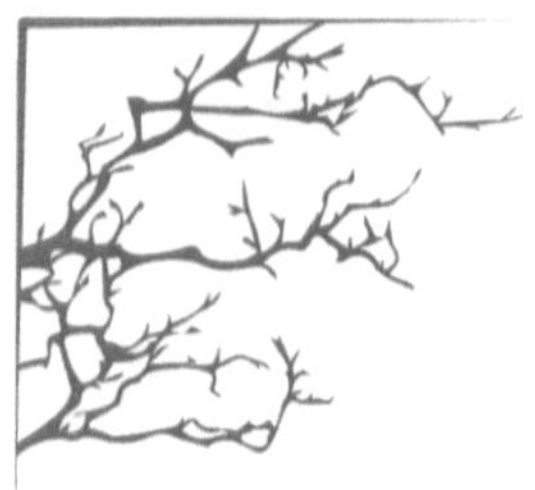

Mothman

The enigmatic Mothman is one of the most intriguing and hair-raising cryptids in modern folklore. The Mothman is often described as a humanoid creature with large wings, reminiscent of a moth, and glowing red eyes. Despite the eerie nature of this legend, it captures the imagination and curiosity of people across the globe.

The origins of the Mothman legend can be traced back to Point Pleasant, West Virginia, in the mid- 1960s. The first notable sighting occurred on November 12, 1966, when five men were digging a grave at a cemetery near Clendenin, West Virginia. They reported seeing a man-like figure with wings flying low from the trees over their heads. Over the next year, more sightings were reported, with the most famous account being on November 15, 1966. Two young couples, Roger and Linda Scarberry, and Steve and Mary Mallette, encountered a large creature with glowing red eyes while driving near an old World War II TNT plant north of Point Pleasant. The creature followed their car, flying at speeds exceeding 100 mph.

As reports of the Mothman sightings spread, the small town of Point Pleasant became the center of media attention. Paranormal investigators, UFO enthusiasts, and curiosity-seekers flocked to the area, hoping to glimpse the mysterious creature. John Keel, a noted journalist and UFOlogist, published a book in 1975 titled 'The Mothman Prophecies', documenting his investigation and suggesting that the Mothman sightings were connected to other unexplained phenomena, including UFO sightings and psychic phenomena. Keel's book was later adapted into a film in 2002, further popularizing the Mothman legend.

One of the most tragic events associated with the Mothman legend is the collapse of the Silver Bridge on December 15, 1967. The bridge, which connected Point Pleasant to Gallipolis, Ohio, collapsed during rush hour, resulting in the deaths of 46 people. Some locals believe the Mothman sightings warned of the impending disaster, adding a layer of ominous mystery to the creature's legend.

The scientific community remains skeptical about the Mothman's existence, attributing sightings to the misidentification of known animals, optical illusions, or hoaxes. Some suggest that the Mothman may be an enormous bird, such as a sandhill crane or a barred owl, with wingspans and reflective eyes that could match eyewitness descriptions.

Despite the skepticism, the legend of the Mothman endures. Point Pleasant has embraced its cryptid celebrity, hosting an annual Mothman Festival that attracts thousands of visitors. The festival features guest speakers, live music, vendors, and a Mothman museum, making it a celebration of paranormal curiosity and local lore.

The Mothman remains a fascinating part of American folklore, symbolizing the fear of the unknown and humanity's enduring fascination with the supernatural. Whether a figment of imagination, a misidentified animal, or something truly unexplained, the Mothman continues to captivate and mystify those who hear its legend.

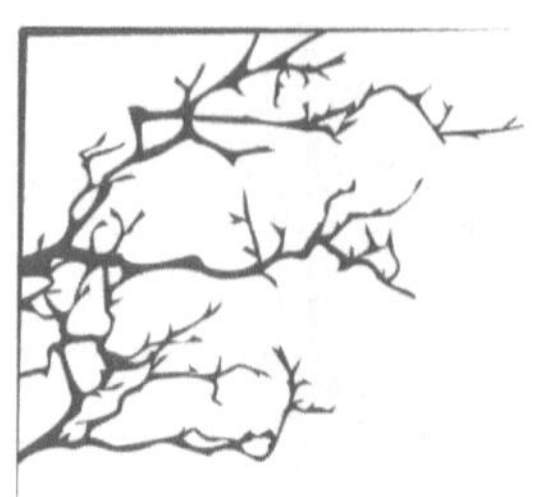

Jersey Devil

The story of the Jersey Devil is one of the most famous cryptid legends from the United States. Nestled deep in the dense forests of Southern New Jersey's Pine Barrens, the Jersey Devil has been a source of fear and fascination for centuries. The creature is described as a flying biped with hooves, often depicted with the body of a kangaroo, the head of a goat, leathery bat-like wings, horns, small arms with clawed hands, and a forked tail. It is said to move quickly and emit a blood-curdling scream that can be heard from miles away.

The Jersey Devil's story has been fueled by various reported sightings over the years. In the early 19th century, Commodore Stephen Decatur is said to have spotted the creature and even fired a cannonball directly at it, but it had no effect. In 1909, the legend gripped the entire region when a wave of sightings was reported over a week. Newspapers of the time were filled with accounts from people who claimed to have encountered the devil. Schools and workplaces were closed as a panic spread, and even police were called in to investigate the strange occurrences.

Scientific investigations and skepticism have done little to quell the enduring legend of the Jersey Devil. Zoologists and cryptozoologists alike have tried to provide rational explanations, suggesting the creature could be a misidentified known animal or even a hoax propagated by those seeking attention or media coverage. Yet, despite these efforts, the mystery of the Jersey Devil remains, enticing enthusiasts and paranormal investigators to venture into the Pine Barrens in search of evidence.

The cultural impact of the Jersey Devil is significant, particularly in New Jersey, where it has become a regional icon. The creature has inspired books, movies, and even a professional hockey team – the New Jersey Devils. Tales of the Jersey Devil are passed down through generations, keeping the legend alive. It is frequently featured in local folklore festivals, Halloween events, and ghost tours, drawing in tourists and enthusiasts from all over the world.

Despite the lack of concrete evidence, the Jersey Devil continues to capture the imagination of those who hear its story. A mix of fear, awe, and the mysterious, it embodies how folklore can evolve and persist in a community's collective memory. Whether a real creature lurking in the shadows of the Pine Barrens or merely a figment of legend, the Jersey Devil remains a fascinating and enigmatic part of American cryptid lore.

Yeti (Abominable Snowman)

The Yeti, also known as the Abominable Snowman, is a legendary creature said to inhabit the Himalayan mountain range in Asia. The origins of the Yeti trace back to ancient folklore and stories passed down through generations, primarily among the indigenous peoples of Nepal, India, and Tibet. Descriptions of the Yeti vary, but generally, it is depicted as a large, ape-like being. It is often described as standing anywhere from six to ten feet tall, covered in fur that ranges from white to brown, which helps it blend into its snowy surroundings. The creature is said to have a massive, strong build, with a face resembling that of a human or an ape, and enormous feet leaving distinctive footprints in the snow.

Famous sightings and reports of encounters with the Yeti began gaining widespread attention in the early 20th century. One of the most renowned reports came from British mountaineer Eric Shipton, who in 1951, claimed to have discovered and photographed large footprints while on an expedition to Mount Everest. These footprints, measuring about thirteen inches in length, were unlike any known animal tracks and ignited global interest and speculation about the existence of the Yeti. Another significant account came from Sir Edmund Hillary and Tenzing Norgay, the first climbers confirmed to have reached the summit of Mount Everest in 1953. Both men reported seeing large tracks that they believed belonged to the Yeti.

Scientific investigations into the Yeti have been conducted, but concrete evidence remains elusive. In the mid-20th century, several expeditions were led by scientists and enthusiasts hoping to find proof of the creature's existence. The most notable of these was the 1957 Slick-Johnson Snowman Expedition, which set out to Bhutan in search of evidence. While the expedition didn't find the Yeti, they collected what they believed were tufts of Yeti hair, which were later analyzed but inconclusive. Genetic testing in recent years, including an analysis conducted by Oxford University and the Lausanne Museum of Zoology, examined samples believed to be from Yetis. Upon closer inspection, most of these samples were found to match the genetic profiles of known animals such as bears and other common wildlife.

However, despite these findings, many believers remain convinced of the Yeti's existence, attributing its elusiveness to the remote and harsh environment in which it supposedly lives.

The cultural impact of the Yeti is profound, particularly in regions where the lore originates. In Nepal and Tibet, the Yeti is a prominent figure in local folklore, often depicted as a guardian of the mountains and forests. It embodies the mystical and unknown nature of the high Himalayas. The creature has also permeated popular culture and media worldwide. From movies and television shows to literature and video games, the Yeti has been an enduring subject of fascination. Films such as 'The Abominable Snowman' (1957) and 'Smallfoot' (2018) have introduced the Yeti to global audiences, while books like 'Tintin in Tibet' have captivated readers of all ages. The Yeti's image as a symbol of the unknown and the human desire to explore and understand the mysteries of the world continues to captivate and inspire curiosity.

Despite the skepticism of the scientific community, the legend of the Yeti lives on. Whether as a mythical guardian of the Himalayas or an unexplained phenomenon, the Yeti represents the allure of the unknown and our unending quest for discovery.

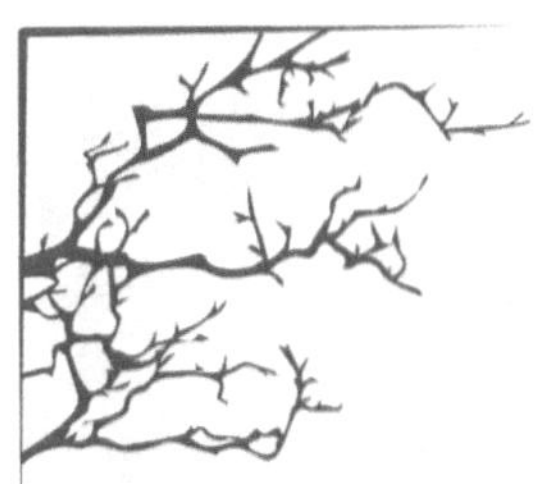

Bunyip

The Bunyip is one of the most intriguing and elusive cryptids originating from Australian Aboriginal mythology. This creature's descriptions vary widely, adding an extra layer of mystery and allure. In some stories, the Bunyip is depicted as a large, lake-dwelling creature with features resembling both a bird and a crocodile. Other accounts describe it as a giant starfish, or even a massive, furry animal of undetermined shape. This ambiguity in appearance has made the Bunyip a rich subject for folklore and legend across Australia.

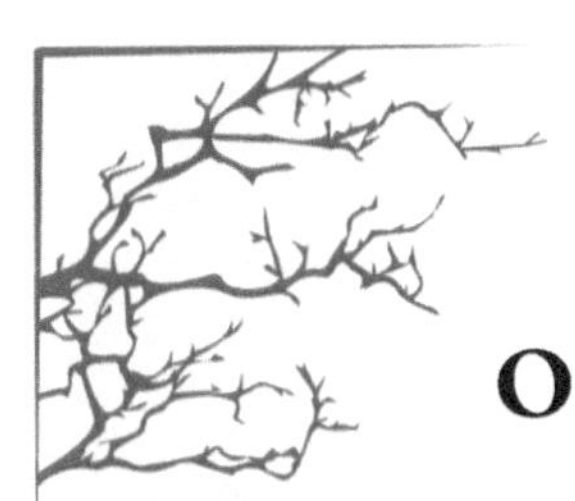

Origins and Description

The term 'Bunyip' is derived from the Wemba-Wemba or Wergaia language of the Aboriginal people of southeastern Australia, and it translates roughly to 'devil' or 'evil spirit'. This cryptid typically allegedly resides in swamps, billabongs, creeks, riverbeds, and waterholes. The origins of the Bunyip legend are rooted deep in the oral traditions of the Aboriginal people, who have passed down tales of this mysterious creature through generations.

The Bunyip is often described as having a horrifying, otherworldly appearance. It is said to have an immense body covered in feathers or fur and a face with prominent, glowing eyes. Some accounts say it has a long neck and a beak akin to a bird's, while others suggest it looks like a giant seal or an overgrown otter. This wild variance in descriptions hints at a conflation of several animals, each contributing characteristics to the myth of the Bunyip.

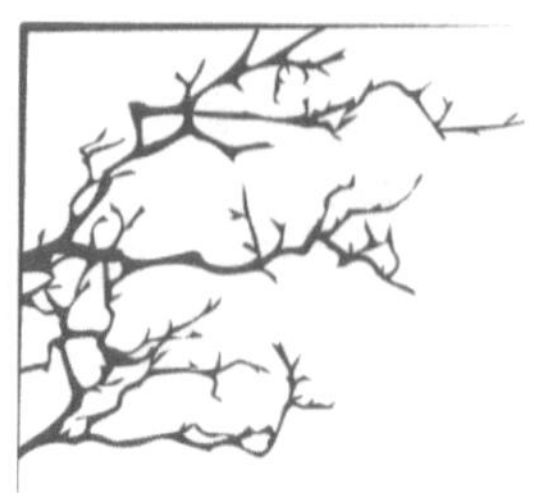

Famous Sightings

Numerous reported sightings of the Bunyip throughout Australia, especially in the 19th and early 20th centuries. One of the most famous cases occurred in 1845 when a strangled party of settlers claimed to encounter a creature near the Murrumbidgee River in New South Wales. They described it as an animal that made a terrifying loud noise and had murdered their livestock.

In the mid-19th century, an actual skeletal discovery fueled the Bunyip frenzy. In 1846, a peculiar set of bones was discovered near Geelong, Victoria. The bones were displayed in Sydney, and they were initially believed to belong to the Bunyip. However, upon further examination by experts, the skeleton was identified as that of a prehistoric marsupial, Diprotodon. Despite this scientific explanation, many people continued to associate the bones with the legendary Bunyip.

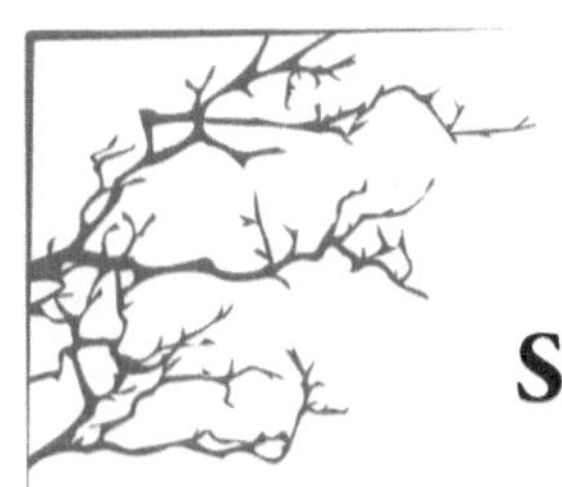

Scientific Investigation

Scientific interest in the Bunyip has been sporadic but persistent. Early European settlers, intrigued by the local legends, sought explanations for what the Bunyip might be. Some theories have proposed that the Bunyip stories may stem from encounters with real but now-extinct Australian animals, such as the Diprotodon or the Procoptodon, a giant kangaroo. Other theories suggest the Bunyip could be a misinterpretation of familiar animals seen under unusual conditions.

In the modern era, cryptozoologists continue to analyze sightings and reports to validate the existence of the Bunyip. They examine historical accounts, assess physical evidence, and explore the potential of unknown animals living in remote Australian waterways. Despite extensive research, no conclusive evidence has been found to substantiate the Bunyip's existence, leaving it firmly in the realm of myth and legend.

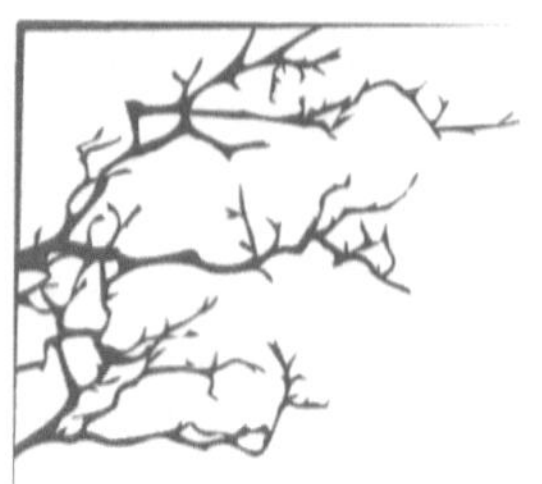

Cultural Impact

The Bunyip holds a significant place in Australian culture and folklore. It has been featured in stories, songs, and artworks, and has even inspired various place names around Australia. The creature continues to captivate the imagination of Australians, remaining a popular subject in children's literature and local storytelling. The legend of the Bunyip embodies the mystique and unexplored nature of Australia's vast wilderness and its unique fauna.

While the Bunyip may forever elude scientific confirmation, its influence on Australian cultural heritage is undeniable. The creature remains an enduring symbol of the unknown mysteries that still inhabit our world, reminding us that there are still many secrets lurking in the wilds of nature.

Kraken: The Legendary Sea Monster

Among all the sea monsters that have swum into our imaginations, none loom as large or as fearsome as the Kraken. This giant cephalopod, often depicted as an enormous octopus or squid, has haunted the minds and seas of sailors for centuries. Tales of the Kraken have been told by maritime folk across numerous cultures, sparking fear and fascination in equal measure. But what are the origins of this monstrous legend, and what makes it so memorable to this day?

The origins of the Kraken legend can be traced back to Norwegian and Greenlandic folklore. Early descriptions from the 18th century describe an animal so large that it could be mistaken for an island. According to these tales, the Kraken would emerge from the depths of the ocean to wrap its monstrous tentacles around ships, dragging them and their unfortunate crews to a watery doom. Described in specific detail in works such as the 1752 book "The Natural History of Norway" by Erik Pontoppidan, the Kraken was said to live off the coast of Norway and Greenland, lying in wait to terrorize sailors.

It's easy to understand the fear that such a creature would inspire. The oceans are vast and unexplored even today, and centuries ago they were dark, mysterious, and full of unknown dangers. In an era when sailing was fraught with peril, the legend of the Kraken wove itself into maritime lore to represent the actual fears faced by those who ventured out to sea.

Famous sightings and records of the Kraken have compounded its legendary status. One of the most notable accounts came from the 13th-century Old Icelandic saga, "Örvar-Oddr". In this saga, the protagonist encounters two sea monsters, one of which resembles the Kraken. Another 18th-century account tells of a bishop in Norway who claimed to have encountered a Kraken so large it resembled a chain of islands, underscoring the awe and fear these stories were designed to evoke.

Given its formidable reputation, it's no wonder that attempts have been made to investigate the Kraken scientifically. Most modern scientists believe that the legend reflects genuine encounters with giant squids (genus Architeuthis), which can grow up to 43 feet (13 meters) or more in length. In recent years, giant squids have been captured on camera in their natural deep-sea habitats, providing a tantalizing glimpse into the potential realities behind the legend. These real sea creatures possess eyes the size of dinner plates, and their long tentacles and powerful beaks could certainly account for the horrifying portrayals of the Kraken in folklore.

From a cultural perspective, the Kraken has permeated literature, film, and popular culture. One need only think of the fearsome creature portrayed in movies such as the "Pirates of the Caribbean" series, where the Kraken is a servant of Davy Jones, or in classic literature like Jules Verne's "Twenty Thousand Leagues Under the Sea". These stories have kept the myth of the Kraken alive and well in the modern imagination, continuing to inspire both fear and fascination.

The mythos of the Kraken emphasize humanity's enduring interest in the unknown. If there are uncharted waters and undiscovered territories, the legend of creatures like the Kraken will persist. The boundaries between reality and myth blur in these dark depths, reminding us of the power of folklore to stir our imaginations and fears.

In conclusion, the Kraken remains one of the most formidable cryptids ever conceived. Its roots in maritime folklore, reinforced by sightings and scientific parallels to real creatures like the giant squid, cement its place in the annals of cryptozoology. Whether regarded as a monster of the depths or a misunderstood natural phenomenon, one thing is for sure: the Kraken's legacy will continue to loom large in our collective consciousness.

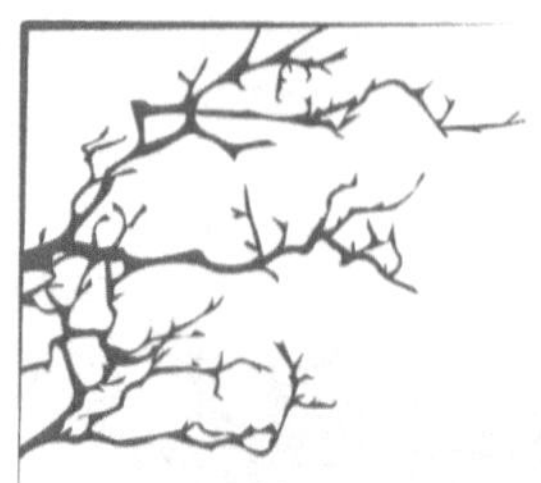

Thunderbird

Thunderbirds are one of the most awe-inspiring and majestic cryptids that have captured human imagination for generations. These legendary birds, often said to possess extraordinary size and power, have roots in the mythology and folklore of many Indigenous tribes across North America, particularly among the Plains and Northwestern tribes. The Thunderbird is revered as a supernatural entity with spiritual solid significance, often associated with thunder, storms, and the heavens.

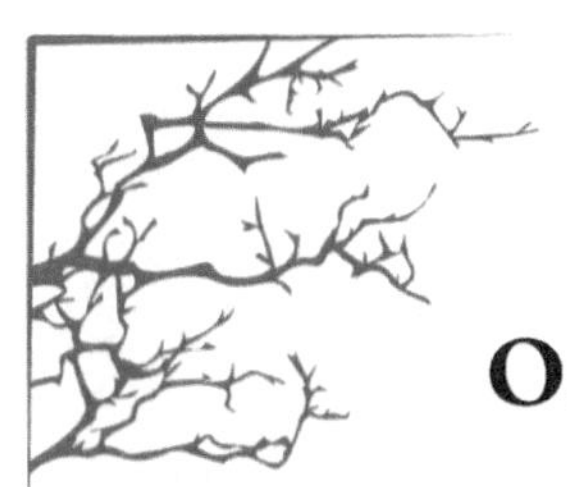

Origins and Description

The Thunderbird's origin can be traced to Native American folklore, where it is described as a giant bird with enormous wings that create thunder as they flap and lightning that shoots from its eyes. Different tribes have varying descriptions, but a common theme is the bird's enormous size, capable of carrying a whale or a human in its talons. Its feathers are said to shine with various colors, and its presence is believed to bring good fortune and formidable storms.

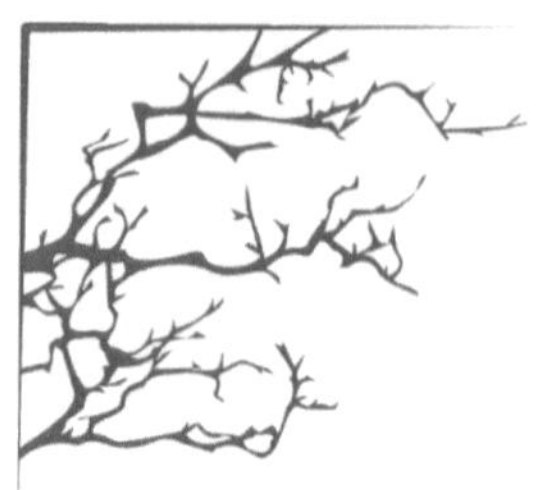

Famous Sightings

Many reported sightings of Thunderbirds throughout history have made them one of the more well-documented cryptids. One of the most famous accounts dates to the late 1800s in Tombstone, Arizona, where two cowboys allegedly shot and killed an enormous bird resembling a prehistoric Pteranodon. The story created a significant buzz, yet no physical evidence was provided, leading to speculation and doubt.

In the 20th century, reports of Thunderbird sightings spanned various states, including Illinois, Pennsylvania, and Alaska. Witnesses often describe the Thunderbird as having a wingspan of over ten feet, sometimes even as large as aircraft. Sightings usually occur before or after thunderstorms, aligning with the creature's mythological ties to weather phenomena.

Scientific Investigations

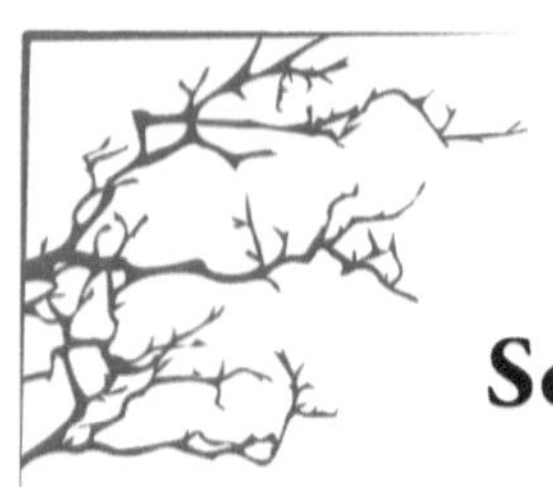

The lack of tangible evidence has always been a significant challenge in verifying the existence of Thunderbirds. Most scientists and researchers remain skeptical, attributing sightings to misidentifications of large birds like condors or eagles, optical illusions, or outright fabrications. Skeptics often note the lack of physical evidence, such as feathers or bones, as a critical point against the Thunderbird's existence.

However, cryptozoologists continue to investigate and collect eyewitness accounts, hoping to prove someday that Thunderbirds are more than a myth. Some suggest that these giant birds could survive members of extinct species like the Teratorns, prehistoric birds that once roamed North America.

Cultural Impact

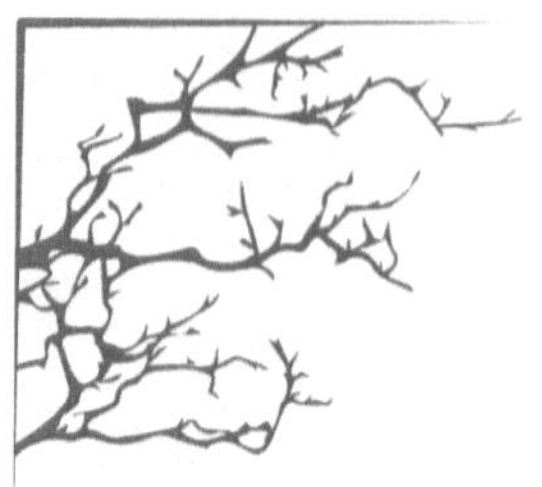

Despite the lack of empirical evidence, Thunderbirds maintain a significant cultural impact, particularly within Indigenous communities. They are celebrated in various art forms, from totem poles and paintings to stories and dances, symbolizing power, protection, and spiritual connection. The Thunderbird also enjoys a place in popular culture, appearing in books, movies, and television shows, often depicted as a creature of immense power and mystery.

The legend of the Thunderbird continues to be a subject of fascination and inspiration. Whether seen as a myth, a symbol, or a potential undiscovered species, Thunderbirds remind us of the power of nature and the mysteries that still await discovery in our world.

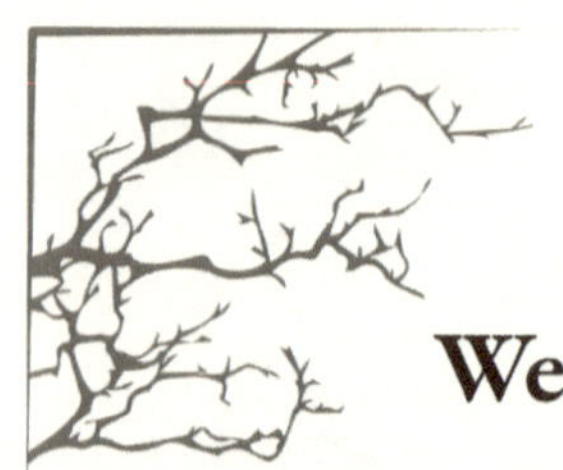

Wendigo: The Spirit of the Lonely Wilderness

The Wendigo is one of the more terrifying cryptids, originating from the folklore of various Native American tribes in the North Canadian and U.S. regions. Known to rove the cold, lonely forests, the Wendigo is described as an evil spirit that possesses humans and turns them into cannibalistic beings. The spirit of the Wendigo is strongly associated with winter, famine, and starvation, which adds an extra chill to its fearsome reputation.

The Origins and Description

The origins of the Wendigo can be found in the lore of the Algonquin-speaking tribes, including the Ojibwe, Cree, and Innu. According to tribal lore, the Wendigo exists somewhere between human and supernatural. Descriptions of its physical appearance vary, but most agree that it is an enormous, gaunt figure with desiccated skin stretched tightly over skeletal features. Some legends describe it with antlers or deer-like features, further emphasizing its connection to the wilderness. The Wendigo's eyes are often said to glow eerily, and its breath is freezing cold. Despite its emaciated appearance, it is said to have a voracious appetite, always craving human flesh.

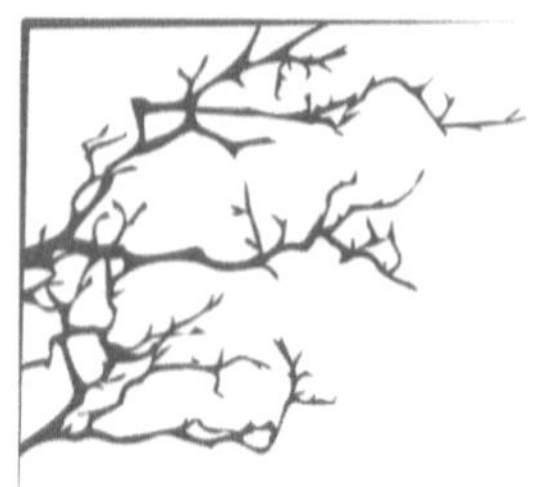

Famous Sightings

Although the Wendigo is primarily a figure from legend, there have been several accounts that claim real-life encounters with this terrifying entity. One of the most famous figures associated with Wendigo lore was Jack Fiddler, an Oji-Cree shaman in the early 20th century, known for his ability to conjure and defeat these creatures. He claimed to have killed 14 Wendigos during his lifetime, a feat that brought him both notoriety and trouble with the Canadian authorities. There have also been sporadic reports from hunters, hikers, and campers who claim to have felt the eerie presence of the Wendigo deep within the forested wilderness, though tangible evidence remains elusive.

Scientific Investigations

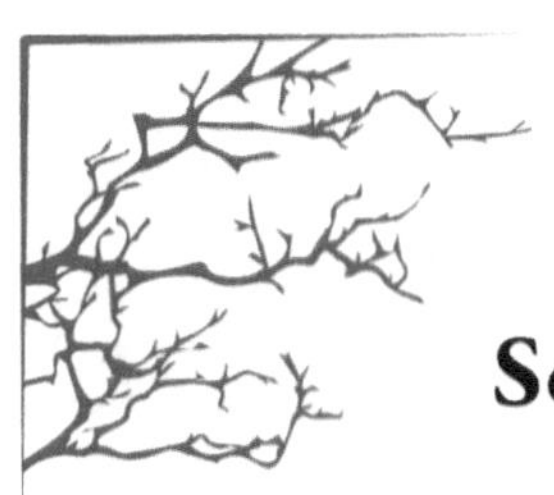

The Wendigo's terrifying nature has made it a subject of interest for both folklorists and psychologists. The term "Wendigo psychosis" has been coined by some scientists to describe a condition where individuals develop an insatiable desire to eat human flesh, often under extreme conditions of starvation. This concept combines the Wendigo legend with documented cases where individuals exhibited cannibalistic tendencies. However, the scientific community remains divided on whether Wendigo psychosis is a genuine cultural-bound syndrome or a form of schizophrenia. Investigations are often inconclusive due to the lack of concrete evidence and the inherent mythological overtones.

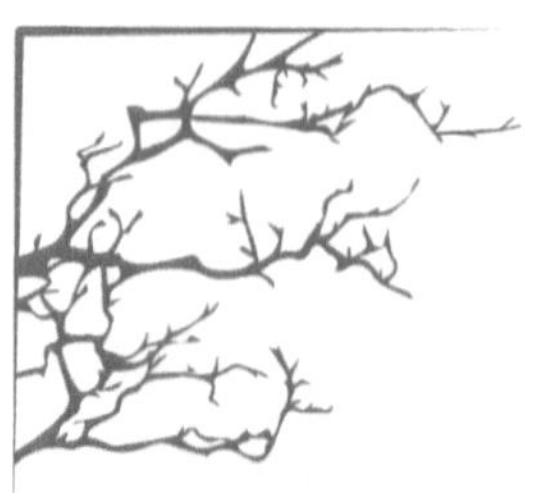

Cultural Impact

The Wendigo has cast a long shadow over popular culture, appearing in various books, movies, and television shows. For instance, Stephen King's novel "Pet Sematary" is often seen as drawing from Wendigo lore, while the monster has also featured in TV series such as "Supernatural" and "Hannibal." Its embodiment of starvation and desperation taps into universal fears, making the Wendigo a compelling figure in horror fiction. The concept of a creature that can possess and transform humans into something monstrous resonates with deeper anxieties about losing one's humanity and succumbing to primal urges.

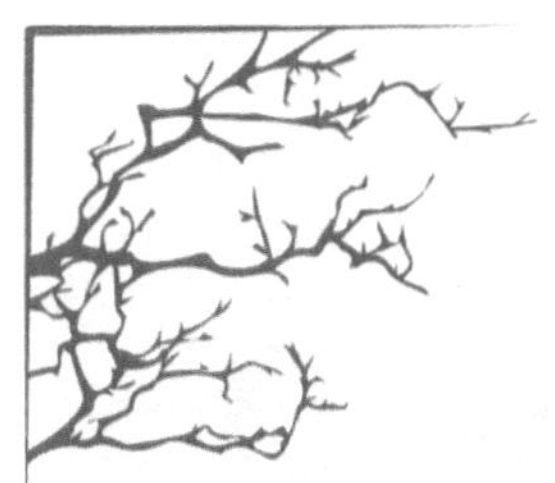

Final Thoughts

While proof of the Wendigo's existence remains as elusive as the creature's, its enduring presence in folklore and contemporary media speaks to its powerful impact on human imagination. Whether seen as a literal monster haunting the forests or a metaphor for the darkness within, the Wendigo remains one of the most spine-chilling cryptids ever conceived. Its tales remind us of the thin line between survival and predation and the terrifying possibility that, under desperate conditions, humanity might slip away, leaving something monstrous in its place.

Concluding Thoughts on Cryptids: Mysteries Yet Unsolved

In exploring the world's most enigmatic creatures, we have journeyed through the lore and legends surrounding some of the most well-known cryptids. From the dense forests hiding Bigfoot to the deep waters concealing the Loch Ness Monster, and the eerie folklore of the Chupacabra and Mothman, each cryptid story carries a unique cultural and scientific significance. We've examined famous sightings that have sparked widespread intrigue and attempts at scientific verification that continue to challenge the boundaries of our understanding. The Jersey Devil, Yeti, Bunyip, Kraken, Thunderbird, and Wendigo each present a fascinating blend of myth and reality that persists in modern culture. This e-book provides a comprehensive overview of these mysterious beings, encouraging a mix of skepticism and wonder. Cryptids remain a captivating part of human curiosity, and their stories symbolize the thrill of the unknown. Ultimately, whether these creatures are real or figments of our imagination, their impact on our collective consciousness is undeniable, keeping the quest for discovery alive and well.

THANK YOU!